WASHINGTON, D.C.
portrait of a city

WASHINGTON, D.C.

portrait of a city

GRAPHIC ARTS BOOKS

The following photographers hold copyright to their images as indicated:
Jon Arnold/DanitaDelimont.com, pages 2, 36–37, 39, 56–57, 72–73, 112;
Bill Bachmann/DanitaDelimont.com, page 33; **Dave Bartruff**/DanitaDelimont.com,
pages 8–9, 30, 31, 43; **Walter Bibikow**/DanitaDelimont.com, page 60; **Don Eastman**,
pages 4–5, 12–13, 34, 38, 48, 67 (repeated on back cover), 98, 99, 104, 105;
Dmitriy Fotiyev, page 106; **David R. Frazier**/DanitaDelimont.com, pages 11a, 87;
Kenneth Ilio, page 17; **Stephen Inguanti**, pages 11b, 19, 20, 22 (all), 23, 32, 42, 46, 47,
52, 53, 54, 61, 62, 63, 65, 84, 88, 89, 91, 92–93, 93, 94, 95, 97; **Ned Messerschmidt**,
page 107; **Michelle Molinari**/DanitaDelimont.com, pages 6, 14; **Connie Ricca**/
DanitaDelimont.com, pages 10, 11c, 21, 24–25, 28–29, 40, 41, 58, 59, 69, 85, 100,
102, 103, 108–9; **Lynn Seldon**/DanitaDelimont.com, page 1; **Keith Stanley**, pages 7,
15, 16, 18, 26, 27, 35, 49, 50, 51, 55, 64, 66, 68, 70, 71, 74, 75, 76, 77, 78, 79, 80, 81,
82, 83, 86 (all), 90, 96, 101, 110, 111, front cover; **Dan Zaharevitz**, pages 44–45.

Book compilation © 2005 by
Graphic Arts Books, an imprint of
Graphic Arts Center Publishing Company
P.O. Box 10306, Portland, Oregon 97296-0306
503/226-2402; www.gacpc.com

Library of Congress Control Number: 2005929667
International Standard Book Number: 978-1-55868-920-6

The five-dot logo is a registered trademark of
Graphic Arts Center Publishing Company.

President: Charles M. Hopkins
Associate Publisher: Douglas A. Pfeiffer
Editorial Staff: Timothy W. Frew, Tricia Brown,
Kathy Howard, Jean Bond-Slaughter
Production Staff: Richard L. Owsiany, Heather Doornink
Cover Design: Elizabeth Watson
Interior Design: Jean Andrews

Printed in the United States of America
Second Printing

FRONT COVER: ❙ Cherry blossoms set off the
555-foot-tall Washington Monument, dedicated in 1885.
BACK COVER: ❙ The Peace Monument stands in front of the Capitol.
◄◄ The White House, originally completed in 1800, was rebuilt and
restored after the British burned it, along with the Capitol, in 1814.
◄ A radiant Capitol shimmers in the low light of evening.
► The Jefferson Memorial was dedicated in 1943, on the
two hundredth anniversary of Jefferson's birth.

▲ Along with numerous other events, the
annual National Cherry Blossom Festival includes
kite flying—within sight of the Washington Monument.
▶ A giant Japanese lantern reaches for a
canopy of cherry blossoms.

◄ The Castle, completed in 1855, was the
Smithsonian Institute's only facility at one time;
now hundreds of museums worldwide are
administered by the Smithsonian.

▲ Displays in the National
Museum of African Art range from
furniture and tools to ceramics and textiles, from
masks to figures and musical instruments.

▲ CLOCKWISE FROM TOP LEFT:
Among Smithsonian exhibits are historical modes
of transportation and weaponry, ranging from ◖ The *Spirit of St. Louis,*
flown by Charles Lindbergh in 1921 in the first solo, nonstop, transatlantic flight; to
◖ a Tomahawk missile, a "smart" weapon with radar guidance, displayed with other missiles; to
◖ a stagecoach that once transported mail, now housed in the Postal Museum.

▶ Donated to the United States in celebration of the nation's bicentennial, the American Freedom Bell has graced the front of Union Station since 1981. The bell is nearly twice the size of the real Liberty Bell, which rests in Philadelphia, Pennsylvania.

◄ The American flag flies before the Washington
Monument. Today's flag has thirteen stripes (for the
original thirteen colonies) and fifty stars (for today's fifty
states). The fiftieth star, for Hawaii, was added on July 4, 1960.
▲ The World War II Memorial was created to honor those who served in
the armed forces of the United States, those who died, and
all those who supported the war effort from home.

15

▲ The Marine Corps Marathon,
which is run each year as a charity outreach,
has helped in numerous causes, ranging from the
fight against autism to aid for the elderly.

▲ The AIDS Memorial Quilt is the
world's largest community arts project.
The quilt's more than 44,000 panels memorialize
the lives of those lost to AIDS.

▲ The white bark of birch trees contrasts with the
delicate pink of cherry blossoms to form a colorful display.
The ambience of historical buildings and memorials, offset by the
beauty of flowering trees and a bright blue D.C. sky,
draws thousands of tourists each spring.

▲ John Parke Custis acquired Arlington in
1778. His granddaughter, Mary Anne Randolph Custis,
married Robert E. Lee in 1831. Since the Civil War, the estate
has been the official burial grounds for those whose
lives have been sacrificed for their country.

▲ The Hirschhorn Museum is the Smithsonian
Institute's Museum of Modern and Contemporary Art.
▶ Artwork is displayed both inside the museum and
outside on the grounds of the Sculpture Garden.

◄ The U.S. Botanic Garden, signed into
existence in 1820 by President James Monroe,
showcases everything from azalea blossoms to exotic orchids.
▲ Located on the National Mall since 1849, it is the nation's
oldest continuously operating botanic garden.
►► The garden encompasses both
indoor and outdoor gardens.

▲ The Rayburn House Office Building,
completed in early 1965, is the most recent of
three offices constructed for the use of the members
of the United States House of Representatives.

▲ At the National Gallery of Art,
an elegant stairway leads to some of the
world's finest paintings, sculptures, and other
art forms that have been created by the
great masters over the centuries.

◄ Restored row houses bring
an upscale look to the revitalized
Shaw neighborhood.

IN CONGRESS, JULY 4, 1776.

A DECLARATION

BY THE REPRESENTATIVES OF THE

UNITED STATES OF AMERICA,

IN GENERAL CONGRESS ASSEMBLED.

WHEN in the Courfe of human Events, it becomes neceffary for one People to diffolve the Political Bands which have connected them with another, and to affume among the Powers of the Earth, the feparate and equal Station to which the Laws of Nature and of Nature's God entitle them, a decent Refpect to the Opinions of Mankind requires that they fhould declare the caufes which impel them to the Separation.

We hold thefe Truths to be felf-evident, that all Men are created equal, that they are endowed by their Creator with certain unalienable Rights, that among thefe are Life, Liberty, and the Purfuit of Happinefs——That to fecure thefe Rights, Governments are inftituted among Men, deriving their juft Powers from the Confent of the Governed, that whenever any Form of Government becomes deftructive of thefe Ends, it is the Right of the People to alter or to abolifh it, and to inftitute new Government, laying its Foundation on fuch Principles, and organizing its Powers in fuch Form, as to them fhall feem moft likely to effect their Safety and Happinefs. Prudence, indeed, will dictate that Governments long eftablifhed fhould not be changed for light and tranfient Caufes; and accordingly all Experience hath fhewn, that Mankind are more difpofed to fuffer, while Evils are fufferable, than to right themfelves by abolifhing the Forms to which they are accuftomed. But when a long Train of Abufes and Ufurpations, purfuing invariably the fame Object, evinces a Defign to reduce them under abfolute Defpotifm, it is their Right, it is their Duty, to throw off fuch Government, and to provide new Guards for their future Security. Such has been the patient Sufferance of thefe Colonies; and fuch is now the Neceffity which conftrains them to alter their former Syftems of Government. The Hiftory of the prefent King of Great-Britain is a Hiftory of repeated Injuries and Ufurpations, all having in direct Object the Eftablifhment of an abfolute Tyranny over thefe States. To prove this, let Facts be fubmitted to a candid World.

He has refufed his Affent to Laws, the moft wholefome and neceffary for the public Good.

He has forbidden his Governors to pafs Laws of immediate and preffing Importance, unlefs fufpended in their Operation till his Affent fhould be obtained; and when fo fufpended, he has utterly neglected to attend to them.

He has refufed to pafs other Laws for the Accommodation of large Diftricts of People, unlefs thofe People would relinquifh the Right of Reprefentation in the Legiflature, a Right ineftimable to them, and formidable to Tyrants only.

He has called together Legiflative Bodies at Places unufual, uncomfortable, and diftant from the Depofitory of their public Records, for the fole Purpofe of fatiguing them into Compliance with his Meafures.

He has diffolved Reprefentative Houfes repeatedly, for oppofing with manly Firmnefs his Invafions on the Rights of the People.

He has refufed for a long Time, after fuch Diffolutions, to caufe others to be elected; whereby the Legiflative Powers, incapable of Annihilation, have returned to the People at large for their exercife; the State remaining in the mean time expofed to all the Dangers of Invafion from without, and Convulfions within.

He has endeavoured to prevent the Population of thefe States; for that Purpofe obftructing the Laws for Naturalization of Foreigners; refufing to pafs others to encourage their Migrations hither, and raifing the Conditions of new Appropriations of Lands.

He has obftructed the Adminiftration of Juftice, by refufing his Affent to Laws for eftablifhing Judiciary Powers.

He has made Judges dependent on his Will alone, for the Tenure of their Offices, and the Amount and Payment of their Salaries.

He has erected a Multitude of new Offices, and fent hither Swarms of Officers to harrafs our People, and eat out their Subftance.

He has kept among us, in Times of Peace, Standing Armies, without the confent of our Legiflatures.

He has affected to render the Military independent of and fuperior to the Civil Power.

He has combined with others to fubject us to a Jurifdiction foreign to our Conftitution, and unacknowledged by our Laws; giving his Affent to their Acts of

◄ A nineteen-foot bronze statue of Thomas Jefferson stands in the memorial erected in his honor. Inscribed near the roof is a quote from the nation's third president: "I have sworn upon the altar of God eternal hostility against every form of tyranny over the mind of man."

▲ The original draft of the Declaration of Independence was written by Thomas Jefferson.

▲ The Jefferson Memorial is nearly hidden
behind a wall of delicate cherry blossoms—and visitors.
► On February 23, 1945, Marines captured the Pacific island of Iwo Jima,
then in Japanese hands. Based on a photograph of the actual event, the statue
depicts the five Marines and one Navy hospital corpsman who raised the
U.S. flag atop Mount Suribachi. The statue is dedicated to all Marines
who have given their lives in defense of their country since 1775.

◄ The idea for a national cathedral was conceived
in 1792, but construction did not actually start until 1907.
The Washington National Cathedral was finally completed in 1990.
▲ Although the nation's first president, George Washington, presided over
construction of the White House, he did not get to live in it. The
privilege of being first to call the White House home fell to
John Adams, America's second president, in 1800.

► Friendship Arch, the largest
single-span Chinese arch in the world,
leads the way to numerous Asian restaurants
and other cultural attractions.

▲ Over the years, Georgetown has cycled and recycled itself
from an upstart community to a hip town to a slum area—and
back to an upscale place to live. Its colorful homes are part of its charm.
▶ Rededicated each year, the Freedom Forum Journalists Memorial honors
reporters, editors, photographers, and broadcasters who have
given their lives in the effort to report the truth.

◄ Old Stone House, built in Georgetown by Christopher Layman in 1765, is
the oldest house—and one of the oldest known structures—in the nation's capital.
▲ Bartholdi Park is named for Frédéric-Auguste Bartholdi (1834–1904), the sculptor of the
fountain at its center. Created for the 1876 International Centennial Exhibition in
Philadelphia, the fountain was placed in its present location in 1932. The
artist's most famous creation is not the fountain, however;
that distinction belongs to the Statue of Liberty.

41

▲ Completed in 1922, the Lincoln Memorial honors
America's sixteenth president and the nation he fought
to preserve. Built to resemble a Greek temple, the memorial has
thirty-six columns, one for each state at the time of Lincoln's death.
▶ Above the statue of Lincoln are the words, "In this temple, as in
the hearts of the people for whom he saved the Union, the
memory of Abraham Lincoln is enshrined forever."

▲ The Key Bridge is named for Francis Scott Key, the man
who wrote "The Star Spangled Banner." Key wrote the words after
anxiously watching the British bombardment of Fort McHenry during the
War of 1812. The bridge, constructed from 1917 to 1923, connects
Virginia to the Georgetown section of Washington, D.C.

▲ The National Herb Garden provides benches
where people can rest, sheltered by a canopy of lush
green overhead. Herbs, by definition, are plants that yield
dyes, fragrances, medicines, and even insecticides—
any use other than for food, wood, or beauty.

▲ A gift to the people of the United
States from the Herb Society of America, the
National Herb Garden was dedicated in 1980. The fountain
is a centerpiece in the garden. All of the garden's
plants, including the trees, are herbs.

▲ The word *Watergate* has entered the national vocabulary
as a term meaning corruption and scandal, yet the Watergate Hotel
is one of the plushest apartment and office complexes in D.C. Here, in
1972, the Watergate burglars broke into the Democratic Party's
National Committee offices. Since then, *gate* added to the
end of any word makes it synonymous with scandal.

▲ The National Archives and Records Administration
houses some five billion paper documents and records along with
millions of photographs, films, videos, and recordings of historical significance.
Among its most famous documents are the Constitution, the Bill of Rights,
and the Declaration of Independence. Outside, in the Sculpture Garden,
the young and the young-at-heart enjoy wintertime ice-skating.

▲ Palestinian women call for peace.
▶ Washington, D.C., is known as a gathering
place for demonstrations—for and
against virtually everything.

◄ Olympic coral is among the many aquatic displays
at the National Aquarium. The aquarium is supported by
donations and admission charges, not the federal government.
▲ Piranhas swim in a tank at the National Aquarium. Though
piranhas have a reputation for being vicious,
in the wild, they rarely attack people.

▲ Alligators patiently wait for prey at the
National Aquarium. Ranging in length from six to
eight inches at birth, the hatchlings, as the babies are called,
are guarded ferociously for the first year by the mother.
Adult male alligators may reach thirteen to fifteen
feet; females, up to about ten feet.

▲ *Leading the charge!* This part of the Ulysses S. Grant
statue depicts horses charging into battle. The general who
became the symbol of Union victory in the Civil War rose
to the rank of commander-in-chief when he was
elected the nation's eighteenth president.

◄ King Street in
Old Town Alexandria presents a
vibrant, picturesque face.

▲ In 1921, Duncan Phillips Jr. opened
the Phillips Collection in his home in memory of
his father and brother. Artists featured in the gallery include
El Greco, Manet, Renoir, Van Gogh, Monet, Degas, Gauguin, and Cézanne.
▶ Constructed in 1909, the building first served as a silent movie house,
then a pool hall before it became Ben's Chili Bowl in 1958.

◄ Now home to the National Building Museum,
the former Pension Bureau building, completed in 1887,
was designed by U.S. Army General Montgomery C. Meigs. The interior
courtyard presents a seemingly endless view of graceful arches.
▲ The Colonial Exhibit at the National Museum of
American History depicts life in the 1700s.

▲ A pair of giant pandas, Mei Xiang and
Tian Tian, are on loan to the National Zoo from the
China Wildlife Conservation Association. On July 9, 2005,
the 250-pound Mei Xiang became the mother of a new
little giant panda named Tai Shan. Newborns usually
weigh in at just three to five ounces.

▲ After years of difficulty in successfully laying
eggs and nurturing chicks, the flamingo flock at
the National Zoo is now healthy and vibrant, raising their
families the way nature designed. Today, visitors
can see a noisy flamingo yard, full of vocal,
active birds—both young and old.

▲ From 1950 to 1953, the United States joined United
Nations forces in Korea to reduce the threat of war worldwide.
The Korean War Veterans Memorial honors those who answered that call.
▶ The Three Servicemen Statue, erected near the Vietnam Wall, honors
veterans of the Vietnam War, fought from 1957 to 1975.

◄ The Old Executive Building is now home to various agencies
of the nation's government, including the office of the vice president.
▲ The forty-four-foot-high white marble Peace Monument commemorates
naval deaths during the Civil War. At the top of the monument, Grief
weeps on History's shoulder. History holds a tablet inscribed with
the words, "They died that their country might live."

▲ Exhibited in the National Air and Space Museum,
the F-4 Phantom II qualified for both land and sea operations.
It was the first multiservice aircraft to fly concurrently with
the U.S. Navy, the Air Force, and the Marines (shown).

▲ The International Spy Museum houses more
than six hundred historical artifacts that help explain
the hows and whys of spying and intelligence operations.
Among the displays are extensive exhibits on terrorism,
the American Civil War, and the Cold War.

▲ The Eastern Market is a vibrant place,
selling produce, meats, fish, and other fresh foods.
▶ Outside the Market, arts and crafts fairs, flea markets,
and farmer's market vendors keep the area alive on weekends.
The original red-brick structure, built in 1873, is still in use.
▶▶ Even traffic adds color to a city that never sleeps,
giving a romantic aura to nighttime D.C.

◀ Although their actual responsibility is to keep peace in
the city, the horse patrol also performs in colorful fashion
in parades, all the while keeping a weather eye out for trouble.
▲ From a quaint, colorful sidewalk rug shop to picturesque memorials,
from contemporary structures to centuries-old homes, from
skyscrapers to stately government buildings, D.C.'s
neighborhoods flaunt their unique personalities.

▲ An uncharacteristically quiet
Dupont Circle Metro Station showcases the
graceful curves incorporated in the design. Dupont
Circle is one of the hubs where the train system
connects with the metro bus system.

▲ Although the food court is empty at the moment,
Union Station sees twenty million people each year. Historically,
its busiest time was during World War II, when as many as 200,000
people passed through in a single day. But after the war, its financial and physical
condition deteriorated as train travel declined. In 1988, the station reopened
with shops, restaurants, and movie theaters occupying the original
building—and a new Amtrak terminal at the back.

▲ The grounds of the Washington
Memorial show their colors in spring, when soft
pinks and brilliant golds contrast with dark green foliage
to brighten the view everywhere one looks.

▲ In the Bethesda neighborhood,
cloud shapes reflected against row house
walls create an intricate collage.

▲ Lights outlining a fresh snow outside
the SunTrust Bank lend a whimsical quality to a
serious business. Average annual snowfall
in the D.C. area is 15.2 inches.

▲ Snow rounds off the sharp edges
of Dupont Circle, giving it a softened look in
twilight's glow. Dupont Circle is a vibrant, happening
place near D.C.'s popular tourist sights.

▲ A Pakistani truck typifies the
ethnic displays exhibited by the Smithsonian.
The intricate graphics of the truck's
grillwork are unsurpassed.

▲ Even more colorful graphics
are depicted on the side panel of the truck.
This kind of artistry gives new meaning
to the term "truck detailing."

▲ An example of the historical craft of
Indian boat making is among the displays in the
National Museum of the American Indian. A prism window
in the atrium casts rainbow colors on people who visit the exhibits.
▶ The museum welcomed its first visitors in 2004. Its wavy walls
evoke the limestone canyons of the American Southwest.

◀ CLOCKWISE FROM TOP LEFT: The Kennedy Center's Performing Arts
for Everyone features a free performance every day of the year. Among the
many Asian performances given by the Silk Road Dance Company in 2002 were
● puppet dancers; ● Chinese opera; ● a cup dancer; ● the Urhoy Choir; and ● mask dancers.
▲ The critters in the Mammal Hall in the National Museum of Natural History look so
real one almost wants to step out of the way. Subjects of the exhibits range
from dinosaurs to microscopic discoveries to a caveman display.

▲ In the Africa Exhibit, a leopard *(Panthera
pardus)* rests beside an impala *(Aepyceros melampus)*
on the branch of a tree. A leopard is able to carry prey
equal to its own weight up a tree to protect it from lions and
hyenas, which can't climb trees to challenge the leopard's success.
▶ A woolly mammoth debuts on the stage of prerecorded
history at the Museum of Natural History.

◄ Franklin D. Roosevelt is the only president ever
elected to four terms (1933–1945), but he died near the
beginning of his fourth term. His vice president, Harry S. Truman,
served out the rest of his term, then was elected to a term of his own.
▲ Waterfalls, lighted at night, cascade over the walls of the Franklin Delano
Roosevelt Memorial, on the Tidal Basin near the National Mall.

◄ The Asian Collections encompass
thirteen acres of the National Arboretum. A red
pagoda sits atop a ridge above China Valley and Asian Valley.
▲ A Japanese iris *(Iris ensata)*, one of a group of
beardless iris, adds its delicate color.

▲ Embracing one of North America's
largest collections of bonsai trees, the National
Bonsai and Penjing Museum opened in 1976. Bonsai is the
process of creating dwarf trees and shaping them by
growing and pruning them in containers.

▲ Hundreds of varieties of blossoms,
ranging from flowering trees to the bright
red corn poppy, brighten the grounds
at the National Arboretum.

▲ As a gift of friendship, in 1912, Japan sent cherry
trees to the U.S. Then, after World War II, in 1952, graftings
from those trees were sent back to Japan to replace trees that had
been destroyed during the war. So a gift given in friendship
came full circle, helping preserve not only the beauty of
Japan but also the beauty of restored friendship.

▲ Sundry varieties of dogwood—ranging from
the flowering dogwood *(Cornus florida)*, native to North America,
to the Chinese dogwood *(Cornus kousa)* to the redosier dogwood *(Cornus sericea)*—
are all part of the National Arboretum's Dogwood Collection. Dogwoods
provide both shade and beauty in gardens across the nation.

▲ In 1932, the Theodore Roosevelt Memorial
Association purchased an island on the Potomac River.
Now renamed Roosevelt Island, it is the site of a memorial in
honor of the twenty-sixth president of the United States.
▶ In a clearing at the center of the island stands a
twenty-two-foot bronze statue of Roosevelt.

◄ A fourteen-foot statue at the
Japanese American Memorial depicts two
cranes ensnared in barbed wire and struggling to get free.
▲ The memorial honors the 120,000 Japanese Americans—men,
women, and children—who spent the war years in internment
camps, as well as the 30,000 Japanese Americans who
served in the U.S. military in World War II.

▲ Edward Kennedy "Duke" Ellington (1899–1974) helped define the word
jazz. A songwriter, composer, and performer, the Duke entertained audiences all over
the world, including performances for President Nixon and Queen Elizabeth II. The mural,
completed in 1997, shows Ellington looking out over the neighborhood where he grew up.

▶ Some 185,000 African Americans fought for freedom, both for themselves and for
others, in the Civil War. A statue in their honor stands in the Shaw neighborhood.

◄ Although the Supreme Court first convened
in 1790, it was not until some 145 years later that the
highest court in the land finally found a permanent home.
Construction on the Supreme Court Building was finished in 1935.
▲ The Old Post Office, completed in 1899, was renovated in
1983 by Arthur Cotton Moore. It now features a food
court, shops, and an entertainment stage.

▲ The Chesapeake and Ohio Canal follows the Potomac River
for about 185 miles from Cumberland, Maryland, to Washington, D.C.
For nearly a century, from 1828 to 1924, the canal served as an important
transportation conduit, mostly hauling coal to the nation's capital.
Hundreds of original structures—locks, lock houses, and
aqueducts—remind one of the canal's original role.

▲ In early spring, pawpaw flowers are just
starting to open along the Chesapeake and Ohio Canal.
Native to North America, the pawpaw tree produces an edible,
delicious fruit. The Chesapeake and Ohio Canal National
Historical Park embraces some of the richest diversity
of plant life east of the Mississippi River.

◄ Schoolchildren enjoy learning history while traveling part of the Chesapeake and Ohio Canal from its Georgetown port in a ninety-foot-long, twelve-foot-wide boat—pulled by a mule at two and a half miles an hour.

◄ Organ pipes at the National Shrine of the
Immaculate Conception are both beautiful and practical.
▲ Stained-glass windows grace the National Shrine,
one of the world's largest churches. Its design is
a mix of Romanesque and Byzantine styles.

111

▲ Moonrise, a setting sun, and the Capitol
create a tranquil scene at day's end.